HARMONY IN LOVE

A 100-DAY
RELATIONSHIP GROWTH
JOURNAL FOR WOMEN

THIS BOOK BELONGS TO:

HARMONY IN LOVE

Introduction to "Harmony in Love" – A Journey Through Relationship Growth

How to Use Harmony in Love Journal – A Guided Journey for Couples

Communication
(Days 1-20)

Trust and Commitment
(Days 21-30)

Emotional Support and Empathy
(Days 31-40)

Conflict Resolution
(Days 41-55)

Quality Time and Shared Activities
(Days 56-70)

Intimacy and Affection
(Days 71-80)

Personal and Relationship Goals
(Days 81-90)

Financial Understanding and Goals
(Days 91-100)

Introduction to "Harmony in Love" – A Journey Through Relationship Growth

Welcome to "Harmony in Love," a purposefully designed 100-day journal for couples seeking to deepen their connection and navigate the complexities of a shared life. This journal is structured to guide you through a sequential journey, addressing key areas fundamental to a healthy and thriving relationship.

The structure of this journal is meticulously designed to guide you through a progressive exploration of both the complexities and strengths within your relationship:

- **Communication:** The cornerstone of any relationship, effective communication sets the stage for understanding and resolving issues.
- **Trust and Commitment:** Building a foundation of trust paves the way for a secure and committed partnership.
- **Emotional Support and Empathy:** These components foster deeper emotional connections, essential for weathering life's challenges together.
- **Conflict Resolution:** Learning to resolve disagreements constructively is crucial for maintaining a healthy relationship dynamic.
- **Quality Time and Shared Activities:** Shared experiences reinforce bonds and create lasting memories.
- **Intimacy and Affection:** Deepening intimacy and expressing affection strengthen the emotional and physical connection.
- **Personal and Relationship Goals:** Aligning individual and shared aspirations ensures that both partners grow together.

- **Financial Understanding and Goals:** Harmonizing financial perspectives and goals can prevent one of the most common sources of stress in relationships.

The Flow and Its Benefits

The journey starts with communication, as it's the bedrock upon which all other aspects of a relationship are built. As you progress, each section builds upon the previous, gradually deepening your connection and understanding. For example, effective communication enhances trust, which in turn creates a safer space for emotional support and empathy. This foundation makes conflict resolution more effective, paving the way for enjoying quality time and deepening intimacy. Aligning goals and harmonizing finances towards the end of the journey helps solidify the partnership's future direction.

Overcoming Challenges and Improving the Relationship

This structured approach is designed to methodically address common challenges in relationships. By focusing on one key area at a time, the journal helps couples develop skills and insights gradually, without feeling overwhelmed.

Each section not only addresses specific aspects of a relationship but also interconnects with others to create a comprehensive improvement. For instance, better communication skills enhance conflict resolution, while trust building fosters a more open and honest exchange about goals and finances.

In summary, "Harmony in Love" is more than just a daily journal; it is a guided path for couples to explore, understand, and grow with each other. Through positive affirmations, thoughtful prompts, engaging activities, and reflective discussions, this journal is a tool for couples to strengthen their relationship and overcome obstacles together, paving the way for a more harmonious and fulfilling partnership.

How to Use Harmony in Love Journal – A Guided Journey for Couples

"Harmony in Love Journal" offers a unique approach to strengthening your relationship through both individual introspection and shared exploration. With each partner having their own journal, the journey is personal yet interconnected, enhancing your bond. Here's how to navigate this journey together:

Individual Reflection

- **Positive Affirmations:** Start each day by reading the positive affirmation aloud or to yourself, setting the tone for a constructive mindset.
- **Daily Prompts:** Respond independently to the day's prompt in your journal, delving into your thoughts, feelings, and perspectives on the theme.
- **Privacy and Respect:** During this stage, respect each other's privacy. Your journal is your personal space for honest self-expression.

Shared Activities and Discussion

- **Engaging Together:** After reflecting individually, come together to share your insights from the prompt, fostering open communication and deeper understanding.
- **Activity Suggestions:** Engage in the suggested activity related to the day's theme. This collaborative exercise is designed to strengthen your bond and apply what you've learned.
- **Adapt and Reflect:** Feel free to adapt the activity to better suit your relationship. After the activity, use the space provided to reflect on your experience.

Regular Check-ins

- **Weekly Reviews:** Dedicate time each week to review your journey. Share significant insights, breakthroughs, or challenges from the past week.
- **Support and Growth:** Use these check-ins to support each other, celebrate your growth, and encourage continual improvement.

Tips for a Successful Journey

- **Consistency:** Engage with your journal daily to fully embrace its benefits.
- **Honesty and Openness:** Approach each entry and discussion with honesty and an open heart.
- **Understanding and Patience:** Acknowledge that each of you may process thoughts and emotions differently.
- **Personalization:** The journal is a guide, but your unique relationship dynamics are key. Personalize the experience to best reflect your journey together.

"Harmony in Love" is more than a journal; it's a tool for nurturing growth both as individuals and as a couple, paving the way for a more harmonious and fulfilling relationship.

COMMUNICATION
(DAYS 1-20)

DAY 1

I communicate
with love and understanding.

Reflect on your communication style and how it differs from your partner's.

Discuss your styles and identify one way each of you can adapt to improve communication.

DAY 2

I listen
with an open heart and mind.

Think of a recent conversation where you may not have fully understood your partner.

_____
_____
_____
_____
_____
_____
_____
_____
_____

Revisit the conversation, practicing active listening by summarizing what your partner said.

_____
_____
_____
_____
_____

DAY 3

I express my needs clearly and respectfully.

Identify a need you have that you find difficult to express.

Communicate this need to your partner, focusing on clarity and openness.

DAY 4

I am attentive to my partner's non-verbal cues.

Reflect on how body language affects communication between you both.

Have a conversation using only non-verbal cues, then discuss the experience.

DAY 5

I approach misunderstandings with patience and clarity.

Recall a recent misunderstanding. What caused it?

Discuss how it could have been avoided and create a plan for future misunderstandings.

DAY 6

I acknowledge and appreciate the positives in my relationship

Think about a positive aspect of your relationship.

Share this with your partner and discuss why it's meaningful to you.

DAY 7

I can discuss difficult topics with courage and calm.

Choose a difficult topic you've avoided discussing.

Have a calm, respectful conversation about it, setting ground rules first.

DAY 8

I express gratitude freely and often.

Identify something your partner recently did that you appreciated.

_____
_____
_____
_____
_____
_____
_____
_____

Express your appreciation and discuss the impact of positive reinforcement.

_____
_____
_____
_____

HARMONY IN LOVE

DAY 9

I am honest and vulnerable in sharing my feelings.

Reflect on a time you weren't emotionally honest with your partner.

Share your true feelings about that moment, focusing on honesty and vulnerability.

DAY 10

I ask questions that deepen our connection.

Think about a topic you'd like to know more about your partner's thoughts on.

Have a conversation using only open-ended questions about this topic.

DAY 11

I balance speaking with listening in our conversations.

Reflect on your balance of speaking versus listening in conversations.

Practice a conversation where you consciously balance these roles.

DAY 12

My non-verbal communication is loving and supportive.

Recall a moment when your partner's non-verbal gesture made you feel loved. What was the gesture?

Share affection through non-verbal actions like smiles, hugs, or a surprise gesture. Reflect on the emotional impact of these silent expressions of love.

DAY 13

I use a tone of voice that conveys kindness and respect.

Consider how tone of voice affects the way you interpret each other's words.

Experiment with saying the same sentence in different tones and discuss the impact.

DAY 14

I communicate effectively, even under stress.

Recall a stressful situation and how you communicated during it.

_____
_____
_____
_____
_____
_____
_____
_____
_____
_____

Discuss more effective communication strategies for future stress.

_____
_____
_____
_____
_____
_____

DAY 15

I show affection
through both my words and actions.

Think about how you prefer to communicate affection.

Express affection in your preferred way, and then share with your partner why this method is special to you.

DAY 16

I respect my partner's boundaries and express my own.

Reflect on a time when your or your partner's boundaries were crossed.

_____
_____
_____
_____
_____
_____
_____
_____
_____

Discuss these boundaries and how to better communicate and respect them.

_____
_____
_____
_____
_____

DAY 17

I apologize
sincerely and forgive genuinely.

Think about a time you owed your partner an apology.

Apologies sincerely, discussing the feelings involved.

DAY 18

I support my partner's dreams and share my own.

Reflect on a personal dream or aspiration you haven't shared much with your partner. Why is it important to you, and what has held you back from discussing it?

Discuss how you can support each other in achieving your dreams.

DAY 19

I learn and grow from our past conversations.

Think about a conversation that had a significant impact on your relationship.

Discuss why this conversation was impactful and what can be learned from it.

DAY 20

I am committed to continually improving our communication.

Identify areas of communication you want to improve in the future.

Create a "communication improvement plan" with steps and goals.

TRUST AND COMMITMENT
(DAYS 21-30)

DAY 21

I build trust through my actions and reliability.

Reflect on what actions or behaviors build trust in your relationship.

Share your thoughts with your partner and give an example of when they demonstrated this behavior.

DAY 22

I show my commitment through daily acts of love and respect.

Reflect on actions that symbolize commitment in your relationship.

Choose one action to demonstrate commitment to your partner and implement it today.

DAY 23

I work towards overcoming barriers to trust with honesty and openness.

Identify a past incident that may have hindered trust.

Have an open discussion about it and ways to rebuild trust moving forward.

DAY 24

Our goals align, strengthening our shared journey.

Reflect on your personal goals for the upcoming year. Consider how these goals complement and align with the future you envision with your partner.

Create a joint goal and plan steps to achieve it together.

DAY 25

I trust my partner deeply and demonstrate it through my actions.

Consider areas where you need to trust your partner more.

Engage in an activity that requires trust, like allowing your partner to make decisions for a shared experience, and discuss your feelings afterward.

DAY 26

Honesty is the cornerstone of our trust and relationship.

Reflect on how honesty impacts trust in your relationship.

Share something with your partner that you've been hesitant to discuss.

DAY 27

I openly share and address my fears and insecurities.

Identify a fear or insecurity affecting your trust in the relationship.

Discuss this with your partner and collaboratively find ways to offer reassurance and address these feelings together.

DAY 28

I celebrate our milestones, cherishing our growth together.

Recall a significant milestone in your relationship.

Celebrate this milestone and discuss how it has strengthened your commitment.

DAY 29

I learn from others to nurture trust and commitment in our relationship.

Think of a couple you admire for their trust and commitment.

Discuss what aspects of their relationship you can incorporate into yours.

DAY 30

I reaffirm my commitment, deeply valuing our bond.

Write down what commitment means to you in this relationship.

_____
_____
_____
_____
_____
_____
_____
_____

Share your writing and discuss ways to continuously reinforce this commitment.

_____
_____
_____
_____

HARMONY IN LOVE

EMOTIONAL SUPPORT AND EMPATHY
(DAYS 31-40)

DAY 31

I understand and respect my emotional needs and those of my partner.

Reflect on what you need most from your partner when you're feeling emotional.

Share these needs with your partner and discuss how each of you can better meet them.

DAY 32

I respond to my partner's feelings with empathy and compassion.

Think of a recent situation where your partner was upset. How did you respond, and how could you have shown more empathy?

Discuss this situation and role-play a more empathetic response.

DAY 33

I am emotionally available and present in our relationship.

Recall a moment you felt deeply heard and supported by your partner.

Have a 'heart-to-heart' where each of you shares a personal story, focusing on active listening and emotional support.

DAY 34

I communicate effectively and respond thoughtfully to emotional cues.

Recall a time when your partner's emotional reaction surprised you.

Discuss how you both can better communicate and respond to these reactions.

DAY 35

I support my partner's emotional growth and celebrate their progress.

Think about an aspect of your emotional self you'd like to develop. How can this growth benefit both you and your relationship?

_____
_____
_____
_____
_____
_____
_____
_____

Share your thoughts with your partner. Together, come up with a specific action or habit you can each adopt to support each other's emotional growth.

_____
_____
_____
_____
_____

DAY 36

I validate my partner's feelings, recognizing their importance.

Think of a moment you felt your emotions weren't validated.

Share this with your partner and discuss how you can better validate each other's feelings.

DAY 37

I handle emotional conflicts with understanding and a desire for resolution.

Reflect on an emotional conflict and how it was resolved.

Discuss what could be improved for future conflicts.

DAY 38

I offer empathy first, understanding its power in healing.

Consider a situation where your partner needed empathy, but you offered solutions instead. How could a more empathetic response have been beneficial?

Revisit the conversation, this time offering empathy instead of solutions.

DAY 39

I share my personal challenges openly, fostering a supportive and empathetic bond.

Reflect on a personal challenge you haven't fully shared with your partner. How does this challenge affect you emotionally?

Discuss this challenge with your partner, asking for empathetic listening rather than immediate solutions.

DAY 40

We cultivate a culture of empathy in our relationship, nurturing a deep and understanding connection.

Reflect on moments when you felt deeply empathized with by your partner. What actions or behaviors fostered this sense of empathy?

Together, select a daily empathetic action to practice and support each other in this commitment.

CONFLICT RESOLUTION
(DAYS 41-55)

DAY 41

I recognize patterns in conflicts and work towards peaceful resolutions.

Reflect on a recent conflict and identify the pattern or trigger that led to it.

Discuss how to avoid or address these patterns in the future.

DAY 42

I respond to conflict with thoughtfulness, not impulsiveness.

Think about how you typically react during a conflict. How could you respond more constructively?

Role-play a past conflict, focusing on responding thoughtfully instead of reacting impulsively.

DAY 43

I embrace compromise to find mutual understanding in conflicts.

Think about a past conflict where a compromise might have led to a better outcome. How could a middle ground have been reached?

Practice compromising by finding a middle ground in a current disagreement.

DAY 44

I prevent conflict escalation by staying calm and composed.

Reflect on a past conflict that escalated. What could have been done differently to maintain calm?

Together, identify early signs of escalation in conflicts and agree on strategies to de-escalate them in the future.

DAY 45

I manage my anger constructively to foster healthy discussions.

Reflect on how you usually handle anger or frustration in conflicts. What techniques have been effective for you?

Next time a conflict arises, consciously apply these techniques and reflect on the outcome.

DAY 46

I am committed to developing my conflict resolution skills.

Identify a conflict resolution skill you'd like to improve.

Work together to develop a plan for improving this skill.

HARMONY IN LOVE

DAY 47

I recognize and mitigate the impact of external stress on our conflicts.

Reflect on how external stressors have previously influenced conflicts in your relationship. What patterns do you notice?

Choose and plan a stress-reducing activity to try together next time you face external stress, aiming to lessen its impact on your relationship.

DAY 48

I learn from past conflicts to improve our future interactions.

Think about a significant past conflict. What key lessons did you learn about yourself and your relationship?

Together, create a brief 'lessons learned' list from this conflict to guide future interactions.

DAY 49

I choose the right time to address conflicts, ensuring a constructive outcome.

Think about an instance when timing affected the outcome of a conflict. Discuss the best times to address conflicts.

Agree on a 'safe time' to discuss difficult topics when both are calm and not preoccupied.

DAY 50

Together, we find solutions that respect both our perspectives.

Reflect on a recent minor disagreement. What differing perspectives were involved?

Work together on a solution for this disagreement and later discuss its effectiveness.

DAY 51

During conflicts, I maintain respectful and clear communication.

Reflect on how your communication style shifts during a conflict.

In your next disagreement, consciously practice your ideal communication style and discuss the experience afterward.

DAY 52

I apologize sincerely and value the power of forgiveness.

Reflect on how you apologize after a conflict. Is there room for improvement?

Practice giving a sincere apology for a past conflict where it may have been lacking.

DAY 53

I balance emotions and logic to resolve conflicts effectively.

Think about a conflict where emotions overruled logic.

Write down logical points and emotional feelings during a disagreement, then discuss.

DAY 54

I strive to understand my partner's perspective in every conflict.

Choose a past conflict and try to understand it from your partner's perspective.

Each partner explains their perspective, while the other actively listens and reflects.

DAY 55

We have a solid plan for resolving conflicts and growing stronger together.

Develop a conflict resolution plan that includes strategies discussed in the previous days.

Role-play a hypothetical conflict scenario using your newly developed plan, then discuss its effectiveness and any adjustments needed.

QUALITY TIME AND SHARED ACTIVITIES
(DAYS 56-70)

DAY 56

We cherish quality time together, making each moment count.

Reflect on your ideal way to spend quality time together. What activities make you feel most connected?

Plan a special day or evening together based on these preferences and spend it without any distractions.

DAY 57

We embrace new experiences, growing together through shared activities.

Think of an activity you've never done together but would like to try.

Research and plan how to engage in this new activity together in the near future.

DAY 58

Our shared memories are treasures of our love.

Think about a moment with your partner that stands out as particularly special. Why does it hold such significance?

Create a simple keepsake, like a drawing or a written note, to symbolize this cherished memory.

DAY 59

Learning together strengthens our bond and broadens our horizons.

Choose a topic or skill you're both interested in but know little about.

Spend time together researching or taking an online class on this topic.

DAY 60

Unplugging from technology, we connect more deeply with each other.

Reflect on how technology affects your interactions and quality time.

Plan a tech-free day where you focus solely on each other.

DAY 61

Cooking together is a recipe for joy and teamwork in our relationship.

Pick a recipe that neither of you has tried before.

Cook this meal together, focusing on teamwork and enjoying the process.

DAY 62

Every outdoor adventure brings us closer to nature and each other.

Discuss your favorite outdoor activities or ones you'd like to try.

Plan and go on an outdoor adventure, such as hiking, biking, or a picnic.

DAY 63

Sharing our interests, we discover new facets of each other.

Reflect on a personal hobby or interest that you haven't shared in-depth with your partner. Why is it important to you?

Spend time engaging in each other's hobbies, showing interest and support.

DAY 64

Dreaming together, we build a vision for our future adventures.

Dream up your ideal vacation. Where would it be, and what would you do?

_____
_____
_____
_____
_____
_____
_____
_____

Create an itinerary for this dream vacation, even if it's just hypothetical.

_____
_____
_____
_____
_____

DAY 65

Movie and game nights are our special moments of fun and relaxation.

Choose a movie you've both never seen or a game you've never played but are interested in.

Have a movie or game night, complete with snacks and a cozy setting.

DAY 66

Exploring cultures together enriches our understanding and appreciation.

Pick a culture or country that fascinates both of you.

Spend an evening exploring this culture, perhaps through food, music, or a documentary.

DAY 67

Creating art together, we paint our love in vibrant colors.

Think about a creative project you can do together.

Engage in a joint art project, like painting, crafting, or building something.

DAY 68

Discussing books and ideas, we engage in intellectual intimacy

Choose a book or a set of articles on a topic of mutual interest.

Read them separately and then have a discussion about your thoughts and insights.

DAY 69

Physical activities together keep our relationship dynamic and healthy.

Select a physical activity or exercise you can do as a couple.

Engage in this activity together, focusing on encouragement and fun.

DAY 70

Celebrating our achievements, we honor the journey we share.

Reflect on recent achievements, either individually or as a couple.

Celebrate these achievements with a special dinner or a small ceremony.

INTIMACY AND AFFECTION
(DAYS 71-80)

DAY 71

I express affection in ways that resonate with both me and my partner.

Reflect on the ways of expressing affection that are most meaningful to you. Why do these particular expressions resonate with you?

Share your preferred expressions of affection with your partner and practice showing affection in those ways for each other.

DAY 72

I embrace physical intimacy as a beautiful expression of our love.

Reflect on what physical intimacy means to you and how comfortable you feel with it.

Share your thoughts and engage in a consensual, intimate activity that you both feel comfortable with.

HARMONY IN LOVE

DAY 73

Sharing personal stories deepens our emotional intimacy.

Reflect on an untold personal story you wish to share with your partner.

Take turns sharing and actively listening to each other's stories.

DAY 74

I appreciate my partner through genuine compliments.

Think about the importance of compliments in your relationship.

Give each other genuine, heartfelt compliments.

DAY 75

Understanding our love languages enhances our bond.

Think about your partner's love language and its role in your relationship.

Express affection in your partner's primary love language today.

DAY 76

Every gentle touch enriches our bond and conveys deep trust.

Reflect on the role and importance of non-sexual touch in your relationship. How does it make you feel connected to your partner?

Spend time cuddling or engaging in affectionate touch.

DAY 77

Revisiting our first moments rekindles our love and affection.

Reminisce about your first date or the first time you knew you were in love.

_____
_____
_____
_____
_____
_____
_____
_____

Recreate aspects of this memorable moment.

_____
_____
_____
_____

DAY 78

I seek daily moments to deepen our intimacy.

Identify ways you can integrate more intimacy into your everyday life.

Implement one of these ways today.

HARMONY IN LOVE

DAY 79

We explore our romantic desires with respect and openness.

Think about a romantic or intimate fantasy you feel comfortable sharing with your partner.

Discuss how you might explore these fantasies together respectfully and consensually.

DAY 80

Planning for intimacy brings excitement and closeness to our relationship.

Reflect on the impact and feelings that come from deliberately planning intimate moments with your partner.

Schedule a romantic or intimate evening together.

PERSONAL AND RELATIONSHIP GOALS (DAYS 81-90)

DAY 81

My personal goals are a reflection of my aspirations, and I cherish the support we give each other.

Identify a personal goal you have and why it's important to you.

Share your goals with each other and discuss how you can support one another in achieving them.

DAY 82

Together, we set goals that strengthen and enrich our relationship.

Reflect on what a shared relationship goal looks like for you and your partner. Why is this goal important for both of you?

_____
_____
_____
_____
_____
_____
_____
_____
_____
_____

Create a plan with steps on how to achieve this goal together.

_____
_____
_____
_____
_____

DAY 83

Our career aspirations complement our life together, balancing ambition with harmony.

Think about your career goals and how they align or conflict with your relationship dynamics. What adjustments might be needed for balance?

Discuss and plan how to balance these aspirations with your relationship.

DAY 84

My personal growth enriches not only my life but also our relationship.

Reflect on an area of personal growth you're working on.

Discuss how this growth impacts your relationship and how your partner can support you.

DAY 85

We align our financial goals for a future that is secure and fulfilling for both of us.

Reflect on your personal financial aspirations and consider how they intertwine with your shared financial objectives.

Together, draft a budget or financial plan that supports your shared and individual goals.

DAY 86

Our health and wellness goals reflect our commitment to a long and happy life together.

Reflect on your personal health and wellness goals and how they contribute to your shared life.

Plan a health-related activity you can do together, like a workout or cooking a healthy meal.

DAY 87

Learning and growing together deepens our bond and broadens our horizons.

Identify a skill or subject you both want to learn more about.

Choose a way to learn about this together, such as taking a class or reading a book.

DAY 88

Our lifestyle goals mirror our shared values and aspirations.

Consider how your personal lifestyle goals complement your relationship.

Together, introduce a small change in your daily life that aligns with these shared goals.

DAY 89

Engaging in our social and community goals enriches our lives and brings us closer.

Consider your goals regarding your social life and community involvement.

Plan an activity that involves socializing or giving back to the community.

DAY 90

Reflecting on our goals, we adapt and grow, always moving forward together.

Reflect on the goals you've discussed over the past days.

Revisit and adjust these goals, setting a date to review them in the future.

FINANCIAL UNDERSTANDING AND GOALS
(DAYS 91-100)

DAY 91

I respect and understand our individual financial values and beliefs, working towards alignment.

Reflect on your core financial values and beliefs. Where do they come from?

_____
_____
_____
_____
_____
_____
_____
_____
_____

Share these with your partner and discuss how they align or differ.

_____
_____
_____
_____
_____

DAY 92

Together, we responsibly assess and manage our financial situation.

Assess your current financial situation individually and as a couple.

Create a joint financial statement, including assets, debts, and expenses.

DAY 93

We set and actively work towards achieving our short-term financial goals.

Identify short-term financial goals for the next year.

Develop a plan with specific steps to achieve these goals.

DAY 94

Our long-term financial planning paves the way for a secure and fulfilling future.

Reflect on your long-term financial goals and how they fit into your shared future vision.

Collaborate to create a long-term financial roadmap, incorporating elements like retirement savings, investment plans, and timelines for major purchases.

DAY 95

Creating a joint budget fosters harmony and respect in our financial decisions.

Share your personal approach to budgeting.

Create a joint monthly budget that reflects both of your spending habits and goals.

DAY 96

We tackle our debts with a unified, proactive approach.

Openly discuss any debts and your feelings about them.

Formulate a joint plan to manage and pay off these debts.

DAY 97

Our career goals and aspirations guide us towards financial growth and stability.

Reflect on how your career aspirations align with your desired income level and overall life goals.

Work together to identify practical steps or actions you can both take to support each other's career and income objectives.

DAY 98

We prepare for the future with prudent financial contingency planning.

Consider potential financial emergencies or changes. How prepared do you feel?

Create an emergency fund plan or review and adjust existing plans.

DAY 99

I am committed to expanding my financial knowledge for our mutual benefit.

Identify areas of financial knowledge you want to improve.

Choose a resource (book, course, article) to learn more about this area.

DAY 100

Regularly reviewing and adjusting our financial goals keeps us on track towards financial well-being.

Reflect on the financial goals and plans you've discussed.

Revisit these goals, make adjustments if needed, and commit to regular check-ins.

CELEBRATING YOUR 100-DAY JOURNEY

As you turn the last page of this 100-day journey, take a moment to reflect on the path you've traveled together. You have shared thoughts, expressed feelings, and embarked on activities that have strengthened the bonds of your relationship. This journey through "Harmony in Love" has not just been about completing daily tasks; it's been a profound exploration of love, understanding, and growth.

Remember, the journey doesn't end here. The insights you've gained, the habits you've developed, and the connections you've deepened are just the beginning. You've laid a foundation that will continue to support and enrich your relationship.

Consider revisiting your favorite affirmations, prompts, and activities from this journal. They can serve as continual guides and inspirations in your relationship. The progress you've made is a testament to your commitment to each other and to building a fulfilling partnership.

We encourage you to celebrate this milestone in your relationship. Acknowledge the effort, love, and dedication it took to reach this point. Your journey together is unique and ongoing, and each day brings new opportunities to grow, love, and understand each other more deeply.

Thank you for allowing **"Harmony in Love"** to be a part of your relationship's story. May the journey ahead be filled with love, joy, and endless discovery.

www.ingramcontent.com/pod-product-compliance
Lightning Source LLC
Chambersburg PA
CBHW071354080526
44587CB00017B/3109